Library of Congress Control Number: 2017907072
ISBN: 978-0-9833841-6-8 - Hard Cover
E-book ISBN: 978-0-9833841-7-5
1st Edition

This is a work of fiction. Names, characters, places and incidents either are the product of the author's imagination or are used fictitiously and any resemblance to any actual persons, living or dead, events or locales is entirely coincidental.

This book was printed by Craft Print Solutions, Singapore

Art production and book layout: Brian Galt at Hang 5 in San Diego

To order additional copies of this book go to www.CaboandCoral.com or contact: Dr Udo Wahn; udo@CaboandCoral.com

Published by CaboandCoral.com. Books with aloha for the ocean-minded child

Dr. Wahn's children's books have been featured in the following publications:
SURFING Magazine, Surfrider Foundation's "Making Waves" magazine, and The Surfer's Journal.

CABO & CORAL MEET A KELP HUGGER

Understanding Climate Change

By
Paolo Cabo Wahn
and
Udo Wahn M.D.

Art by
Jennifer Belote

Dedication

Dedicated to Mother Earth! We pledge to protect and act to save our lovely planet and encourage others to do the same.

'Shakas' 

"The ocean seems so vast that human behavior cannot affect it. But it is not true! Cabo and Coral discover and explain with the help of an unusually long-lived and eloquent octopus how the negative effects of human behavior can be felt all over the planet from the tropical ocean to the Arctic and to the African savannah. And the children end with a message of hope and actions anyone can take."

-Mark Spalding, President, The Ocean Foundation

Acknowledgments

Thank you F**ormer Vice President Al Gore** for providing me training by way of your Climate Reality Project. The training was a life changing event that compelled me to team up with my son Paolo Cabo to act in combating climate change.

Here's to **Greg Hodgson**, CEO of Reef Check.org for his review of the manuscript and valuable scientific knowledge that aided in making this work scientifically legit!

We really appreciate you **Mark Spalding**, President of the Ocean Foundation for your review of the manuscript, excellent suggestions and kind words!

Wow! What a talented artist you are **Jennifer Belote!** You are so passionate about the environment and the welfare of animals. It shows in your art. And we love that you are so incredibly easy to work with!

A shout out to **Brian Galt**, my surfing buddy for 42 years who really knows his way around a computer when doing graphic design. He has expertly put together all 6 of my children's books.

Hey, **Joshua May**, Climate Reality Project mentor! I love your quote: "Alone a drop, together a tide!"

Many mahalos to my wife, **Aleida Wahn** for being a supportive wife and mother as Paolo Cabo and I worked on this project, and for editing the manuscript and making sure all text was fully justified.

PREFACE

An octopus was playfully swimming on a beautiful reef. He was happy until he got stuck in a fisherman's net. The fisherman pulled him up, thinking he just had caught a lot of fish. When he reeled the net up, he was surprised to see an injured octopus. Concerned, the fisherman rowed back to shore and called for a sea life rescue ambulance.

The paramedics gave a pain reliever to the octopus. He fell asleep in an instant. He slept peacefully in the ambulance, not knowing where he was going. When he woke up, he realized he was enclosed in an aquarium. In a panic, he hugged some kelp, which made him feel safer and more comfortable. The attendants decided to name him Kelpy. Kelpy didn't like being in the aquarium. He knew in his mind that he would only stay there for a little while and then try to escape.

Yet years later, Kelpy is still in the aquarium! He is super sad. He remembers the beautiful reef he used to live on and longs to return to it.

It was a flourishing coral reef, where the sun would shine on the calm waters of his habitat. Vibrant fish would swim in and out among the coral heads in this peaceful place. Lobsters crawled on the ocean floor, when not hiding from predators. Seals came up onto the rocks in the reef, and basked in the sun. The coral reef slowed the waves, allowing for a calm area inside the reef. Surfers would surf across the reef. Warm waters flowed back and forth onto the reef, leaving many fish comfortable swimming there. Everything was perfect for all the life forms, such as the coral, algae and the sea creatures.

Kelpy misses the reef so much now that he will take any opportunity to leave this aquarium. How far will he go?

"I just love surfing after a long day at school. It makes me feel so alive and my mind refreshed!" exclaimed Coral. Cabo adds, "It is such a beautiful day to share waves with our friends. But, it is so strange that it is fall and it is so hot! Just like summer. What's up with that?"

Coral explains, “I learned in my science class that the climate around the world is changing dramatically and causing a lot of difficulties for many populations.”
“Like what? ” Cabo asked.
“Let me share what I learned this week,” Coral said. “Ready for this?” she teased. “Cabo, let’s stop by the aquarium on our way home from surfing and I’ll explain.”

The attendant is feeding the sea life in the huge tank through an open lid. Cabo and Coral love to check on Kelpy the octopus and try to cheer him up. He is often sad that he has spent so many years recovering at the aquarium after being injured in the fisherman's net. Their visit brings a warm smile to Kelpy's face. They often find him hugging the kelp like it's his security blanket.

Late that night Kelpy notices that the lid on the tank was left open. “Now’s my chance to escape!” says Kelpy to himself. He slithers through the opening and down the outside of the tank. He is not quite sure where he will end up but he decides to slip through the drain in the floor. Octopuses don’t have skeletons so they can squeeze into impossibly tight spaces. As soon as he enters, he slips down the slimy drain that seems like an endless water slide and finds himself emerging from…….

….a storm drain pipe at the beach! Stoked to be free after all these years, he explores the coral reef and is heartbroken at what he finds. The once colorful reef is pale and deserted. He cries when he recalls how the reef was once teeming with sea life. Turn the page to see what he remembered about his home and how it had appeared. Then come back to this page and color the reef back to life!

Later, Kelpy learns what has happened over the many years while he was stuck in the lonely aquarium. It turns out that many of the things that people all over the world have been doing have caused too much carbon dioxide to build up in the air. That in turn has made the ocean water too acidic and too warm.The air has gotten too warm also. All that change is unhealthy for the coral and the life forms that depend on a healthy reef.

Warmer waters cause the algae that give the coral its magical colors to be expelled from the coral leaving the coral white or bleached. The coral also need calcium to build and maintain a sturdy foundation. Acidification of the ocean waters interferes with that process leaving the coral brittle. Shellfish shells are also weakened. This all spells tragedy for the coral reef.

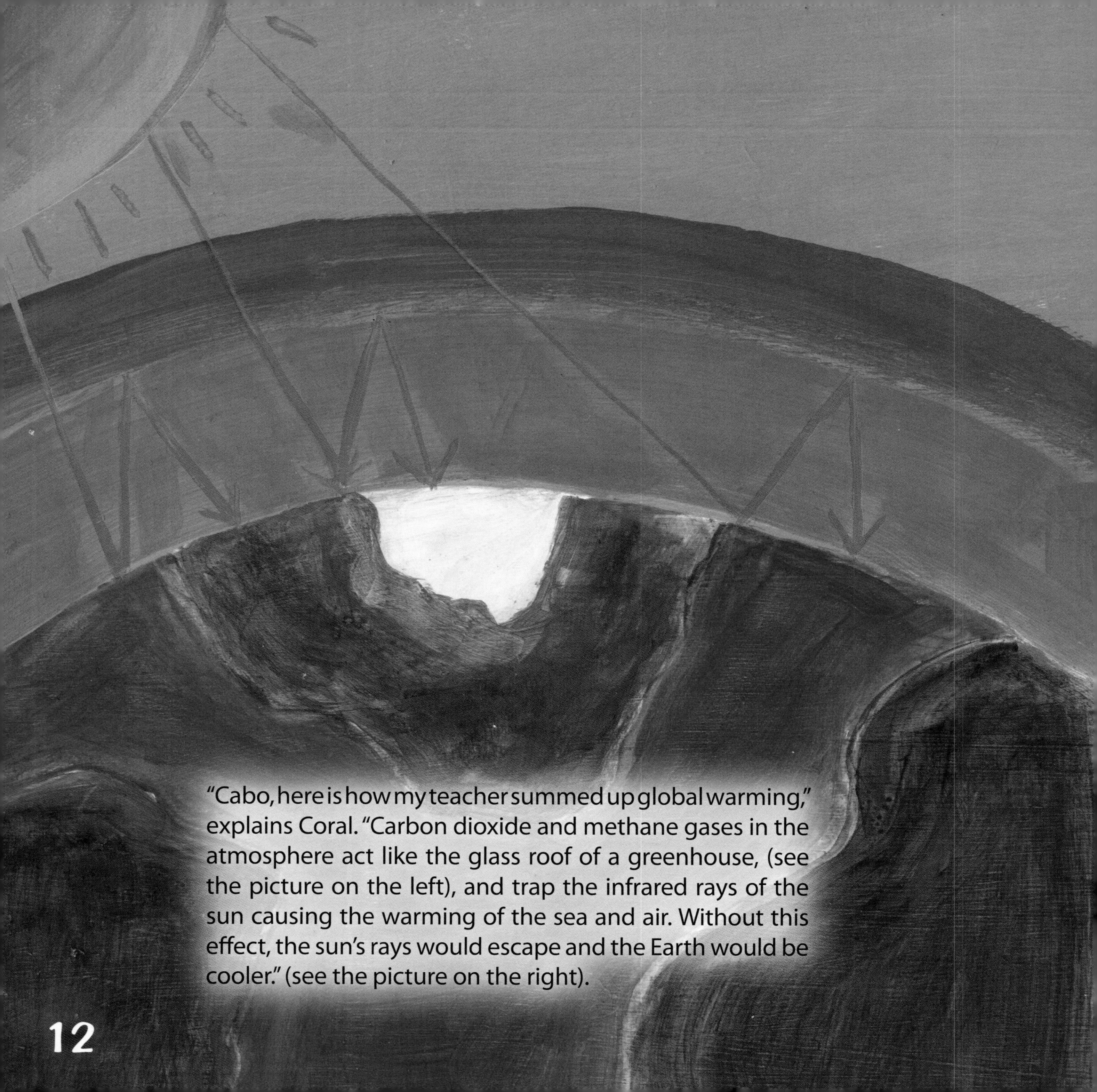

"Cabo, here is how my teacher summed up global warming," explains Coral. "Carbon dioxide and methane gases in the atmosphere act like the glass roof of a greenhouse, (see the picture on the left), and trap the infrared rays of the sun causing the warming of the sea and air. Without this effect, the sun's rays would escape and the Earth would be cooler." (see the picture on the right).

"This manner of warming is called the greenhouse effect. I learned that there are many sources for greenhouse gases. Carbon dioxide (CO_2) is released through exhaust from cars, trucks, and factories burning oil, gas, or coal; and from wildfires burning forests. Methane gas is released by wetlands, and by human activities such as raising livestock, fossil fuel mining, and building landfills. Cooling chemicals in refrigerators and air conditioners can also affect global warming."

"Oh my Coral! Look who is on your surfboard! It's Kelpy!" shouts Cabo over the sound of the crashing waves. Coral shrieks, "YIKES!" Kelpy tries to calm Coral by gently whispering, "Don't be afraid. I have three hearts so I am full of love! I will not hurt you!" Kelpy tells them about his risky escape.

It doesn't take long for Kelpy to fit in because Cabo and Coral practice living Aloha in their lives. Living Aloha means that they are kind to others, and that they share and respect the environment.

One of the other surfers let Kelpy use her surfboard and she pushed Kelpy into a wave so he could surf with Cabo and Coral.

Kelpy shouts out with glee, “This is such a thrill! I never thought in my wildest dreams that I would ever be surfing! Yahoo!” He adds, “I have watched many surfers glide by from below and was mesmerised by them.” Feeling stoked, Kelpy exclaims, “Let’s do this again and again!”

Coral goes on to share more about global warming and its effects. "Cabo, the melting ice in the arctic is causing a slow rise in sea levels and as a result it is increasing coastal erosion and flooding. This has left some Inuit settlements facing destruction."

"Inuit, means 'The People' and they are the original inhabitants of the Artic." Coral adds, "The loss of arctic ice is terrible for wildlife and people such as the Inuit who need the ice to go on their hunts for food and to survive. Wildlife can be left stranded and die. Sea level rise eventually affects us all!"

Turn the page and see what a healthy polar region should look like.

"Cabo, I also learned that the changing climate has created havoc with our planet's usual weather," Coral explained. "Severe droughts, raging storms and wildfires are becoming much more frequent and causing humans and wildlife to die or suffer."

"Trees without enough water cannot fight off disease or keep pests such as the bark beetle away. Drought, disease, and pests kills the trees which makes it easier for forests to catch fire."

"Watering holes like those in Africa that animals in the wild depend on dry up.
You look really sad Cabo, but don't despair, there are things that we can do to make a big difference and alter the course of these unhealthy changes that mankind has created and that are affecting the whole world."

"There is hope Cabo! There is always hope!"

Turn the page to see what the African savanna should look like, then come back to this page and color me back to life!

Cabo and Coral are super happy to know that they can make a difference in stopping the destructive climate changes. Kelpy is thrilled to hear this too! "Coral, I can't wait to learn more about this when I study climate change in my class!" adds Cabo.

Kelpy takes a break from surfing and does what he finds really amusing and that is watching Cabo and Coral slide by together overhead on a wave!

After a simply amazing day, Cabo's mom and dad, Slim and Layla, drive up in their electric van and picnic on the shoreline. Slim and Layla have brought fresh squeezed juices and yummy snacks.

Meanwhile they all watch gleefully as Kelpy gulps down a huge clam that he snagged off the ocean floor. Kelpy offers them all a bite of the raw clam, but they all take a pass.

“I like mine cooked, Kelpy!” says Coral with a tone of yuck! Cabo adds, “ Kelpy is happy as a clam! Wait, I take it back. I bet the clam is not happy at all right now!”

As they wrap it up for the day, they reflect back on what they have learned and they all agree that that they have a newfound confidence in making wonderful changes to save our planet. How COOL is that!

Things That You And Your Family Can Do To Stop Climate Change:

Adapted from the film featuring Former Vice President Al Gore, An Inconvenient Truth

Find out who your elected leaders are and ask them to vote for climate action

Insist that the USA be part of international efforts to address climate change

Walk, bike, carpool or use public transportation

Ask your parents to consider buying a hybrid or electric family car, or even a car that gets better gas mileage

Capture carbon by planting trees

Reduce, reuse, recycle, and refuse

Take your reusable water bottles, utensils and bags with you everywhere

Say "No Thank You" to plastic straws

Ask your parents for help in asking your utility for an energy audit of your home

See how much money can be saved by using less electricity in your home

Ask your utility if they offer renewable energy and if not, why not?

Consider a plant-based diet, or even "Meatless Mondays" for the whole family.

Consider an "Ocean Friendly Garden" (www.Surfrider.org)

Put your knowledge into action!

Are you ready to change the way you live?

"Alone a drop, together a tide!"
- Joshua May

Appendix-
We took the liberty of mixing ecosystems while illustrating, simply to make some of the scenes more visually appealing. For example, while algae is common on coral reefs, kelp is not normally found on coral reefs but there are exceptions. The same holds true for sea lions and seals. Corals are animals but their outer tissue (skin) is inhabited by microscopic algae that are symbiotic. The coral provides nutrients and a safe place to live for the algae while the algae carry out photosynthesis and provide sugar to the coral. So, corals are partly solar powered!

GLOSSARY

Acidification - The process of becoming acid

Algae - A plant that lives in water and has no roots, leaves or stems

Bark beetle - A beetle attracted to weakened trees, which then kills the trees

Captivated - Attracted and held the interest of someone

Carbon dioxide (CO_2) - A gas produced by burning oil, gas, coal, wood and other compounds and by respiration of humans and other animals

Climate change - Global warming and climate change are terms for the observed century-scale rise in the average temperature of the earth's climate system and its related effects

Corals - Animals whose outer skin is inhabited by microscopic algae that give the coral their color

Coral bleaching - Coral forces out colorful algae when water is too warm. This leaves coral white or "bleached"

Drought - A period of unusually low or no rainfall

Erosion - The gradual destruction of something or slow changing of land forms by water or wind or other natural processes

Expel - To force out

Fossil fuels - Fuels like coal or gas formed from the remains of ancient living organisms

Havoc - Widespread destruction

Ice cap - Ice cover over a large area, especially at the north and south poles

Infrared rays - An invisible wavelength of radiation just longer in length than red in the visual spectrum

Green or renewable energy – The terms for electricity and other energy uses that come from sources that can be replenished or are not used up by making energy such as wind, waves, tides, sunshine, and the tapping of earth's natural temperatures (geothermal)

Greenhouse gases - Gases such as CO_2, methane, water vapor, ozone and chlorofluorocarbons that absorb infrared radiation, named for the "greenhouse effect" as described on page 13

Methane - The main component of natural gas and often found with oil and coal deposits. It is also released from decomposed plant or other organic compounds as found in marshes and coal mines. When livestock pass gas, it is methane, a more potent greenhouse gas than CO_2!

Ocean acidification - The ocean becoming more acidic due to the uptake of CO_2 from the atmosphere

Ozone - A toxic gas formed from oxygen by electrical discharges or Ultraviolet (UV) light. A layer of ozone in the upper atmosphere protects life on earth by absorbing high energy solar UV radiation

Personification - Giving something that is non-human, human characteristics. Like Kelpy!

Photosynthesis - The process that plants use to make food from CO_2 and water which generates oxygen (O_2)

Predators - An animal that lives by killing and eating other animals

Reef - A ridge of coral, rock, or sand just below the surface of the ocean

About Paolo Cabo Wahn

Paolo is a student at Earl Warren Middle School in Solana Beach, California. He loves math, robotics, chess, playing tennis and piano. He makes his parents very proud with his accomplishments, like getting straight A's and being a very kind and sensitive guy! He is passionate about changing the direction of our planet's climate.

Paolo and his dad are pictured here at Jalama Creek as it empties into the Pacific Ocean. Jalama is a very special place for the Wahn family.

About Udo Wahn M.D.

Udo is a retired physician living aloha in idyllic Del Mar, California with his wife Aleida and their son Paolo Cabo. He serves as a volunteer on the Executive Committee for Surfrider Foundation where he is the liaison to the S.T.O.P. Coastal Climate Impacts Committee. He trained under Nobel Peace Prize Winner **Former Vice President Al Gore** for the Climate Reality Project. His favorite things to do include surfing, running, mountain biking, camping, and watching silly sitcoms with his family to end the day on a fun note.

Udo is pictured here on the Great South Bay, which lies between his hometown of Sayville, Long Island and Fire Island, New York.

About Jennifer Belote

Jennifer is a member of ocean conservationist Wyland's prestigious Ocean Artists Society. She provided art for Cabo & Coral Reef Explorers and Cabo & Coral Dog Days of Summer. Jennifer is also the founder and operator of: http://thepetscene.com. The premier website for pet owners and businesses.

Paolo and Jennifer pictured in Jennifer's art studio.

About Kelpy (and octopuses in general)

Did you know that octopus stems from the Greek word meaning eight feet? Interestingly, six of these are considered arms that the octopus uses for eating and propulsion. Two legs allow it to move over ground. Do you wonder how Kelpy was able to squeeze his way through the drain? An octopus does not have a bony skeleton so it can squeeze through tight spaces. They have three hearts! They defend themselves by camouflage and can transform to look like a lionfish. They are very fast at escaping danger and have an ink sac that can squirk dark ink to elude predators.

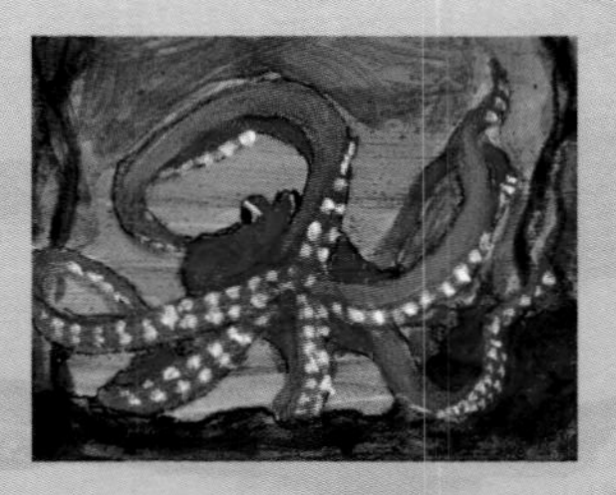